HOW TO ATTRACT YOUR DESIRED CHANGE

THE BEST WAY TO GET THE CHANGE YOU DESIRE FROM GOD

Evangelist

Harrison Johnson Uche

Copyright © 2016. All rights reserved.

No part of this publication may be reproduced, stored in a retrieval system or transmitted in any way by any means, electronic, mechanical, photocopy, recording or otherwise, without the prior permission of the author except as provided by USA copyright law.

All characters appearing in this work are fictitious. Any resemblance to real persons, living or dead, is purely coincidental.

The opinions expressed by the author are not necessarily those of Revival Waves of Glory Books & Publishing.

Published by Revival Waves of Glory Books & Publishing

PO Box 5961 Litchfield, Illinois 62056 USA

www.revivalwavesofgloryministries.com

Revival Waves of Glory Books & Publishing is committed to excellence in the publishing industry.

Book design Copyright © 2016 by Revival Waves of Glory Books & Publishing. All rights reserved.

Published in the United States of America

Paperback: 978-1-68411-037-7

Table of Contents

Chapter One 4

Chapter Two 15

Chapter Three 29

Chapter Four 42

Chapter Five 53

Chapter Six 69

Chapter Seven 82

Chapter Eight. 95

Chapter Nine 110

Chapter One

> Matthew 11 V 28-30: Come unto me, all ye that labour and are heavy laden, and I will give you rest. Take my yoke upon you, and learn of me; for I am meek and lowly in heart: and ye shall find rest unto your souls. For my yoke is easy and my burden is light.

Jesus made this call over two thousand years ago, knowing full well that a lot of people are so confused and tired of their present condition and need God to intervene and deliver them else they may end up hurting themselves and die without remedy.

And from all indications, is never the perfect will of God for his children to stay so long in a particular problem without receiving a solution and a way out any problem or challenging facing them and that is why he made a provision of escape through his son Jesus Christ.

> John 3V35-36: The Father loveth the Son, and hath given all things into his hand. He that believeth on the Son hath everlasting life: and he that believeth not

the Son shall not see life; but the wrath of God abideth on him.

Making it possible for whosoever that obeys the son to be made free or receive whatsoever thing that he/she will ask or seek from the father.

John 14 V 12-14 Verily, verily, I say unto you, He that believeth on me, the works that I do shall he do also; and greater works than these shall he do; because I go unto my Father. And whatsoever ye shall ask in my name, that will I do, that the Father may be glorified in the Son. If ye shall ask any thing in my name, I will do it.

But that will only be on the condition that you must keep his commandments because without being obedient to his commandments he can never show himself so great in your situation.

John 15 V 12- 17 This is my commandment, That ye love one another, as I have loved you. Greater love hath no man than this, that a man lay down his life for his friends. Ye are my friends, if ye do whatsoever I command you. Henceforth I call you not servants; for the servant knoweth not what his lord doeth: but I have called you friends; for all things that I have heard of my Father I have made known unto you. Ye have not chosen me, but I have chosen you, and ordained you, that ye should go and bring forth fruit, and that your fruit should remain: that whatsoever ye shall ask of the Father in my name, he may give it you. These things I command you, that ye love one another.

From the above scripture, you will understand that for God to choose and promise to make all you are asking available to you, it must be for the promotion and growth of his kingdom only.

Meaning that whatsoever thing you are asking from God, if is not in line to promote his kingdom will be wasting of your time and energy which you may final not receive at the end.

Christ's instruction is that you love one another, because without loving others you cannot promote his kingdom as he wants it and by so doing it will be so difficult for you to receive anything or the change you desire from him.

It's the perfect will of Jesus that you receive all that you ask from God, that is why Jesus said that in verse 26 of the same John 15 that he will send a comforter that will abide with you forever to teach you all things including how to achieve whatsoever thing or change you desire in any area of your life.

The comforter, which is the Holy Spirit of God, is the father that will live in you and will not be far from you and if you choose to listen to him he will teach you how to receive your desire change, in other to use it and promote the kingdom of God when you receive such change.

So many Christians today think that God does not answer their prayers to give them their desire change so quick, some people might even ask "am I not a child of God" filled with the Holy Spirit, why is it that I have fasted and prayed for this or that change to happen in my life but without result.

The problem is not that God does not answer prayers but until your desire change becomes in line with his program which is to promote his kingdom with such blessings before he can give them to you.

So many people today are looking for change but they have refused to change in other to allow their desire change to come. Even when the Holy Spirit of God is telling them to change or to amend some areas of their life but they refuse to listen and choose to believe whatsoever they like.

And their desire change can never come until they accept to change their character or their mindset. So many Christians in the churches today are busy complaining or crying to God to change their situation, they are looking unto God for a change in the area of their finance, marriage, health and they believe God to answer their prayers and cause their desire change to happen to them.

So many of them have prayed and become feed up, some people are already offended at God and have arrive at the conclusion where they believed that maybe God does not want to answer them or maybe is not yet time for God to answer them but in the book of, Ephesians 3 v 20: Now unto him that is able to do exceeding abundantly above all that we ask or think, according to the power that worketh in us.

The bible said now, confirming what we read in John 14 V 13: If ye shall ask any thing in my name, I will do it now and not tomorrow. It is the perfect will of God to grant whatsoever change you desire to you without delay. God is interested in changing any ugly situation that devil is using to torment your life, family, marriage, finance, health, business and wants you to live above all the operations of devil and his agents.

He promises to grant the change that you are asking now, meaning that you will have whatsoever request or change you need from God in any area that you wants it according to the power that works in you. Note that when he said according to the power that works in you, the scripture is talking about the Holy Spirit of God in you.

That means for you to receive whatsoever change or thing that you desire from God you need to ask the Holy Spirit to direct you on how to ask for it.

> *John 6 V 26: Jesus answered them and said, Verily, verily, I say unto you, Ye seek me, not because ye saw the miracles, but because ye did eat of the loaves, and were filled.*

Jesus made that statement during one his earthly sermon to the crowd because he knew that so many of the people do not want to receive the word of God and change from their sinful way rather they want to receive God's blessing to go and enjoy in their sin.

That is the state of so many Christians today and that is what is delaying their suppose desire change.

There are two types of Christians in the church today. People who came to serve God because they reorganized him as their God indeed and they have vowed to serve and follow him, the way he is and the next set is the people that reorganized God as their creator and know that he can do all things but they are not fully ready to obey him or keep his commandments, all that matters to them is his blessings, they want God's blessing to go their way. They want to live in promise land with Egyptian mentality.

This type of people is in church but they don't want to involve themselves in any department of the church, they don't want to give anything for the growth of the kingdom of God. They cannot afford to contribute anything like their time, idea, finance or energy.

They cannot afford to invite others to church or tell others what God is doing his church, even when God blesses them, they can never allow others to know, so they will always eat their testimony because they do not want to get involve deeply in the work of God in the church. All that matters to them is for God to bless them and grant their desire change in the area of their marriage, finance, and health etc. , so that they can go back and continue in their sinful way. They want to receive from the kingdom of God to promote the kingdom of darkness. All they think or care is how to receive from God without having his word in their heart

> *Psalms 119 v 130: The entrance of thy words giveth light; it giveth understanding unto the simple.*

People like this in most cases does not want to sit down and listen to the word of God in the church or like to study the word of God on their own, they are only after miracle that they want to receive from God and if the miracle fail to come they will begin to complain but unknown to them that the guild line to receive their desire change will only come from the word of God.

The psalmist makes us to understand that the entrance of God's word produce light, meaning for God to grant your desire change, the word has to mingle with your spirit and change your life first before your desire change will show forth.

For you to receive your desire change, you have to accept the word of God first, allowing it to give your spirit man a new mindset and change your way of thinking before it will produce whatsoever change you desire or what the word says about you.

Choose not to listen to the word will make it impossible for you to receive your desire change.

Whenever you don't want to listen and obey God in the area of your life, be prepare to suffer attacks from the devil and his agents in that area because your desire change will not come to you no matter how you cry or complaining.

> *James 4 V3: Ye ask, and receive not, because ye ask amiss, that ye may consume it upon your lusts.*

When your desire change is not line to promote the kingdom of God, you will not receive such change from God. The bible attracts this reason to the fact that, you want to satisfy your lustful desire and not to promote the kingdom of God. And God will not grant any desire change that you will use to promote the kingdom of darkness and that is why he said that you fail to receive because you want to consume it upon your lust and all fleshly lust are the works of the devil.

> *Galatians 5 v 19-21: Now the works of the flesh are manifest, which are these; Adultery, fornication, uncleanness, lasciviousness, Idolatry, witchcraft, hatred, variance, emulations, wrath, strife, seditions, heresies, Envyings, murders, drunkenness, revellings and such like: of the which I tell you before, as*

> *I have also told you in time past, that they which do such things shall not inherit the kingdom of God.*

So if your desire change is for you to use it on any of the above mentioned characters, understand that you will not receive such change because God will not grant it until you change your mindset and desire those things that will promote the kingdom of God.

And for you to desire to promote the kingdom of God with your desire change you must allow the Holy Spirit to fill and direct all your doings and your prayers, if not you can never ask aright.

> *Galatians 5 V16 This I say then, Walk in the Spirit, and ye shall not fulfil the lust of the flesh.*

It is important to understand that God is able and willing to give you more than whatsoever thing you want in life as long as you will use it to promote his kingdom, whenever you have the mindset that you are not going to use whatsoever change you receive from God for your lust of the flesh then Holy Spirit will take over you and cause such change to happen quickly to you. It is the perfect will of the father to give whatsoever desire change you want now.

Ephesians 3 v20: Now unto him that is able to do exceeding abundantly above all that we ask or think, according to the power that worketh in us,

Chapter Two

PROMOTING THE GROWTH OF HIS KINGDOM ONLY

> *1 Corinthians 3v21: Therefore let no man glory in men. For all things are yours;*

Financial Breakthrough, Forgiveness, Healings, Fruit of the womb, life partner, Peace of the mind, Joy and Comfort you desire in your marriage, business and family are already yours in Christ.

All your heart desire or change you need in life is already given freely to you according to,

> *1 Corinthians 2v12: Now we have received, not the spirit of the world, but the spirit which is of God; that we might know the things that are freely given to us of God.*

The above verse made it clear that your desire change and many more of God's blessings have been freely given to you and that God has given you his spirit that will teach you how to receive them and use it to promote the Kingdom of God when you receive them.

It is the perfect will and original plan of the Father to give whatsoever thing that you desire in life as his child. Whatsoever blessing that the Father has is for his children but you must be ready to use them and promote his Kingdom before he will give it to you.

> *Matthew 7v6: Give not that which is holy unto the dogs, neither cast ye your pearls before swine, lest they trample them under their feet, and turn again and rend you.*

Our Lord Jesus Christ made this statement to his listeners to let them know that God cannot release your desire change if it is not in line with his will and plan, which is to promote his kingdom on earth. Until your desire change reflects to the perfect will of the Father which is to promote his kingdom on earth, God cannot grant you such change, no matter how long you pray for such change to come.

If the reason you desire God's healing is for people that wished for your death to see that they are not your God. You desire your healing so that you can put them to shame, sorry God might not heal you. But God only want to heal you so that you will testify to the world that God can still heal sickness even today.

If the reason to ask God for husband is for people that laughed at you or for people that think that you cannot get married because of one thing or the other to be put to shame. You are still prolonging your marriage because God will not grant your request for partner until you understand that the reason he is given you a husband or partner is for you to be committed more in his Kingdom and raise children that will represent him on earth.

If you want God to bless you with a good job, nice car, good house let be that your aim is to use such blessing to promote the Kingdom of God because if you aim is to use it and show your enemies or those that might have mocked at you before that you have arrived, you are making a great mistake because God might not answer you speedily and you may end up being offended thinking that God does not answer your prayers,

> *Matthew 6v33: But seek ye first the kingdom of God, and his righteousness; and all these things shall be added unto you.*

Jesus made this statement, meaning that you must first of all seek to promote the kingdom of God with the desire change you want, before God will release them to you. It is the perfect will of God for you to receive all the change you desire in any area of your life even more than what you may ask.

> *Ephesians 3v 20: Now unto him that is able to do exceeding abundantly above all that we ask or think, according to the power that worketh in us.*

God will release more than you ask, if the power that is working in you is the zeal to promote his Kingdom, where we read said he will perform more than what you are asking now. It is very interesting to know that God is interested in releasing your heart desire if you wish to promote his kingdom on earth with your desire.

So change your desire change and let it be God "I will use my desire change to worship you in fullness." Please provide a new car for me, so that I may take my entire family to church every Sunday.

God give me financial breakthrough so that I may contribute in expanding your church project that I may visit the homeless and support the missionaries around the world then God will answer you without delay because at this point, you are not praying to consume it in your lustful passion anymore rather to promote his kingdom first.

> *James 4v3: Ye ask, and receive not, because ye ask amiss, that ye may consume it upon your lusts.*

And for your lustful passion and desire to be destroyed you must allow the Holy Spirit to teach you thereby understanding that lustful desire is against the will of God and that God cannot be moved whenever he sees them in you.

> *Romans 6v6: Knowing this, that our old man is crucified with him, that the body of sin might be destroyed, that henceforth we should not serve sin.*

Whenever you allow the Holy Spirit to bring you to the knowledge where you will understand that you cannot please God in your carnality it will open you to understand that God does not grant the request of a sinner easily.

> *Proverbs 15 v8: The sacrifice of the wicked is an abomination to the Lord: but the prayer of the upright is his delight.*

This will open you to the understanding to know that whenever you are praying in a lustful desire that your prayer is considered in the sight of God as that of the sacrifice of wicked that is an abomination unto God.

And this will also open you to understand and to know that the reason or why most of your previous prayers have not been answered, is simple because they are not in line to promote God's kingdom which is the basis or the only thing that matters most to God and what he wants from you.

> *James 4v3: Ye ask, and receive not, because ye ask amiss, that ye may consume it upon your lusts.*

When Apostle James made this statement, he was not talking to unbelievers but to believers and to all that has covenant in Christ today who share the same faith assuring them that whatsoever thing they ask the Father in line with his perfect will shall be given to them.

Maybe before he wrote that to them many of them might have been complaining as you are doing without knowing why God has not answered their prayers.

Understand that God can only be attracting to your situation, when the change you are asking is to promote his kingdom and glorify his name in your life. If the change you desire is to revenge your enemies, know that God is not interested in such desire, rather He will step aside and wait till you change your mentality.

> *Matthew 6v33: But seek ye first the kingdom of God, and his righteousness;*

and all these things shall be added unto you.

Without the mentality to seek promote God's kingdom with your desire change, your prayer will not be answered.

> *1 Samuel 1 v 1-28: Now there was a certain man of Ramathaim–zophim, of mount Ephraim, and his name was Elkanah, the son of Jeroham, the son of Elihu, the son of Tohu, the son of Zuph, an Ephrathite: And he had two wives; the name of the one was Hannah, and the name of the other Peninnah: and Peninnah had children, but Hannah had no children. And this man went up out of his city yearly to worship and to sacrifice unto the Lord of hosts in Shiloh. And the two sons of Eli, Hophni and Phinehas, the priests of the Lord, were there. And when the time was that Elkanah offered, he gave to Peninnah his wife, and to all her sons and her daughters, portions: But unto Hannah he gave a worthy portion; for he loved Hannah: but the Lord had shut up her womb. And her adversary also provoked her sore, for to make her*

fret, because the Lord had shut up her womb. And as he did so year by year, when she went up to the house of the Lord, so she provoked her; therefore she wept, and did not eat. Then said Elkanah her husband to her, Hannah, why weepest thou? and why eatest thou not? and why is thy heart grieved? am not I better to thee than ten sons? So Hannah rose up after they had eaten in Shiloh, and after they had drunk. Now Eli the priest sat upon a seat by a post of the temple of the Lord. 10 And she was in bitterness of soul, and prayed unto the Lord, and wept sore. And she vowed a vow, and said, O Lord of hosts, if thou wilt indeed look on the affliction of thine handmaid, and remember me, and not forget thine handmaid, but wilt give unto thine handmaid a man child, then I will give him unto the Lord all the days of his life, and there shall no razor come upon his head. And it came to pass, as she continued praying before the Lord, that Eli marked her mouth. Now Hannah, she spake in her heart; only her lips moved, but her voice was not heard: therefore Eli thought she had been drunken. And Eli said unto her, How long wilt thou be drunken? put away thy wine from thee. And Hannah answered and said, No, my lord, I am a woman of a sorrowful spirit: I have drunk neither wine nor strong drink, but have poured out my soul before the Lord. Count not thine handmaid for a daughter of Belial: for out of the abundance of my complaint and grief have I spoken hitherto. Then Eli answered and said, Go in peace: and the God of Israel grant thee thy petition that thou hast asked of him. And she said, Letthine handmaid find grace in thy sight. So the woman went her way, and did eat, and her countenance was no more sad. And they rose up in the morning early, and worshipped before the Lord, and returned, and came to their house to Ramah: and Elkanah knew Hannah his wife; and the Lord remembered her. Wherefore it came to pass, when the time was come about after Hannah had conceived, that she bare a son, and called his name Samuel, saying, Because I have asked him of the Lord.

And the man Elkanah, and all his house, went up to offer unto the Lord the yearly sacrifice, and his vow. But Hannah went not up; for she said unto her husband, I will not go up until the child be weaned, and then I will bring him, that he may appear before the Lord, and there abide forever. And Elkanah her husband said unto her, Do what seemeth thee good; tarry until thou have weaned him; only the Lord establish his word. So the woman abode, and gave her son suck until she weaned him. And when she had weaned him, she took him up with her, with three bullocks, and one ephah of flour, and a bottle of wine, and brought him unto the house of the Lord in Shiloh: and the child was young. And they slew a bullock, and brought the child to Eli. And she said, Oh my lord, as thy soul liveth, my lord, I am the woman that stood by thee here, praying unto the Lord. For this child I prayed; and the Lord hath given me my petition which I asked of him: Therefore also I have lent him to the Lord; as long as he liveth he shall be lent to the Lord. And he worshipped the Lord there.

From the above scripture, you will understand that God promptly refused to answer Hannah until she came to herself and changed her prayer topic and said "Oh Lord if you look on my affliction and bless me with a child, I will give him back to you"

Understand that Hannah has been coming to the same house of God for so many years but she has been complaining to God because all her mates have been blessed with so many children and that they are mocking her because of her inability to conceive. Meaning that the reason she was asking for a child was to prove to her mockers that she has arrived and for the world to know that Hannah can conceive and have a baby.

Still in all her complains and cries she could not attract the change she desire from God because God does not respond to prayers that does not promote his kingdom. Until when her prayer becomes in line with the perfect will of God which is to promote the kingdom of God on earth.

This is a woman who has been praying one particular prayer for some many years without change, she has been experiencing the same presence of God for all these years without solution to her problem, despite the fact that in the presence of God every issues of life is been settled still the presence of

God that Hannah enjoys every year did not solve her problem or attract God to grant her the change she desire, until the day she understood her mistake and decide to use the change that she will receive from God to promote his kingdom and she changed her prayer request to:

"Oh Lord if you look on my affliction and bless me with a child, I will give him back to you"

This simple prayer turns her situation around and attracts God to change her situation.

So many Christians today are facing a lot of difficulties which has lasted long. They are like Hannah; they have experienced one particular problem for many years and have been praying one particular prayer without receiving solution or answer to such prayer.

They came to church with the problem and have been there for so many years without change, why because the change they desire in their heart is not in line with God's will and plan.

And they have not sat down and ask the Holy Spirit to reveal their problem or solution to them. Understand that God is willing to change an ugly situation that comes against any child of God.

> 2 Thessalonians 1v 6: Seeing it is a righteous thing with God to recompense tribulation to them that trouble you;

It is the perfect will of God that you receive your desire change or to deal with whatsoever thing that has been bothering you. The only problem remain is, will you allow the Holy Spirit to teach you how to change your prayer topic or have you vowed to use such change for the growth of the kingdom of God.

Affliction is not supposed to rise up the second time against any child of God as the word of God said in the book of Nahum 1v9: What do ye imagine against the Lord? he will make an utter end: affliction shall not rise up the second time.

All the problems or issues of life are what our Lord Jesus paid for and they are not to supposed to be a problem to any child of God or for Satan to use it to hold you bound again as a child of God.

> 1 Corinthians 2 v12: Now we have received, not the spirit of the world, but the spirit which is of God; that we might know the things that are freely given to us of God.

The only problem limiting you from receiving your desire change is your ignorance to know that you need to decide to use any blessing or change you receive from God to promote his kingdom. When you come to this knowledge nothing will hold you're pray request from God because your prayer will attract God into your request.

Chapter Three
SELF-WILL

Self-will is another big factor that can cause your desire change in life not to come to you easily.

> *Proverbs 16v2: All the ways of a man are clean in his own eyes; but the Lord weigheth the spirits.*
>
> *1Samuel 2v3: Talk no more so exceeding proudly; let not arrogancy come out of your mouth: for the Lord is a God of knowledge, and by him actions are weighed.*

Self-will is that action that you take outside the will of God. Whenever you refuse to allow the Holy Spirit to teach you on how to submit to the will of God at all time and in everything you do and in every area of your life, you will lose direction and be far from the track in whatsoever thing you are doing in life thereby receiving your desire change will be impossible to you because you cannot enjoy the continued presence of the Father that comes from doing his will, instead you will be working in yourself will and can never rely on the Holy Spirit to teach you on how to be obedient to God in that area in order to receive from him.

> *Romans 6v12-14: Let not sin therefore reign in your mortal body, that ye should obey it in the lusts thereof.Neither yield ye your members as instruments of unrighteousness unto sin: but yield yourselves unto God, as those that are alive from the dead, and your members as instruments of righteousness unto God. For sin shall not have dominion over you: for ye are not under the law, but under grace.*

Self-will will make your lustful desire to control your heart, thereby making your request or desire change to centered on your lustful emotions only, causing the Holy Spirit that will grant such request to you to be far from you. Because you cannot be working in your self will and please God.

Romans: 8v5-8: For they that are after the flesh do mind the things of the flesh; but they that are after the Spirit the things of the Spirit.

For to be carnally minded is death; but to be spiritually minded is life and peace.

Because the carnal mind is enmity against God: for it is not subject to the law of God, neither indeed can be. So then they that are in the flesh cannot please God.

Self-will is your thoughts and your ways which are not the thought of the Lord; the Bible said that there are ways that seem good in the eyes of men but the end thereof is destruction. That is to say that most at times thing you might be fighting for or complaining so much to have now might be good to you today but not at long run and God who is all knowing God, that knows from the beginning to the end will be holding you back to avoid mistake and to protect you from gross harm.

Some of the requests might be right but not good at present, so God will keep it, to give them back to give it to you in future after He might have trained you on how to handle such change when they comes your way.

And at this point of training what is expected of you is to wait patiently in prayer and giving thanks to God because you know that he will do it for you at his time. But because of yourself-will you will start complaining and thereby provoked God to anger.

> *Psalm 106v25-26: But murmured in their tents, and hearkened not unto the voice of the Lord. Therefore he lifted up his hand against them, to overthrow them in the wilderness:*

In your self-will, you might size and see God as your mate without knowing it, you see God as whom you can force to do things your own way and not according to the will of the Holy Spirit.

Self-will is the totality of Satan's nature therefore it should not be allowed to exist in your life as a Christian or whenever you are on your way to receive your desire change from God.

> *Romans 12v2: And be not conformed to this world: but be ye transformed by the renewing of your mind, that ye may prove what is that good, and acceptable, and perfect, will of God.*

The above scripture made such warning because whenever you allow your fleshly will to control your heart or desire, you are automatically yielding yourself to devil and to avoid that, you need to renew your mind with the word of God.

Note! There are people piloting the affairs of this word, the scripture called them the rules of this world, they are agents of demonic kingdom, they are promoting the kingdom of darkness and their work is to make you to be self-willed, so that you cannot please God, as your desire change will not come to you.

They use self-will to take God's time in your life; they are the one who told you that time is money, knowing very well that if you give God your time, he will bring money, their aim is to make you use your time in pursuit of worldly processions thereby money will run from you.

> *Matthew 6v33: But seek ye first the kingdom of God, and his righteousness; and all these things shall be added unto you.*

They know very well that the moment you agree with the world of God and allow the Holy Spirit to direct you on how best to seek the kingdom of God with your time that your desire change will come to you and you will not lack any more in life.

And that is why they are making everything possible to disconnect you from God and to connect you with worldly passion, just to make you poor and easy to control.

You have to bear in mind that whatsoever thing that the world offers you is to make you busy and occupy, so that you can leave God behind. Self-will is those dominate factors that are so much important to you as a person, which the world is offering in exchange for your soul and spiritual life.

> *Luke 9v23-26: And he said to them all, If any man will come after me, let him deny himself, and take up his cross daily, and follow me. For whosoever will save his life shall lose it: but whosoever will lose his life for my sake, the same shall save it. For what is a man advantaged, if he gain the whole world, and lose himself, or be cast away? For whosoever shall be ashamed of me and of my words, of him shall the Son of man be ashamed, when he shall come in his own glory, and in his Father's, and of the holy angels.*

Self-will can also be called self-righteousness, doing what men called tradition, church, school, government says rather than what the spirit of God says.

This has made many Christians to tell you proudly that this is the way we do it here in this church and not how the Holy Spirit says but our church constitution. And this sole reason has made many Christians and churches not to work in the spirit; they are working to please men rather the Holy Spirit.

Working in the way they are patterned by the rulers of this world which are controlled by the devil rather than how the Holy Spirit wants them.

And with this pattern it will be very difficult to receive your desire change from God because you will always be mindful of what the world is offering thereby you will be struggling to do what the Holy Spirit of God is saying in any situation and that is what the devil and his agents want and why he does not want you to rely on the Holy Spirit for direction, which will help you to all things.

> *Psalm 84v4-12: My soul longeth, yea, even fainteth for the courts of the Lord: my heart and my flesh crieth out for the living God. Yea, the sparrow hath found an house, and the swallow a nest for herself, where she may lay her young, even thine altars, O Lord of hosts, my King, and my God. Blessed are they that dwell in thy house: they will be still praising thee. Selah. Blessed is the man whose strength is in thee; in whose heart*

are the ways of them. Who passing through the valley of Baca make it a well; the rain also filleth the pools. They go from strength to strength, every one of them in Zion appeareth before God. O Lord God of hosts, hear my prayer: give ear, O God of Jacob. Selah. Behold, O God our shield, and look upon the face of thine anointed. For a day in thy courts is better than a thousand. I had rather be a doorkeeper in the house of my God, than to dwell in the tents of wickedness. For the Lord God is a sun and shield: the Lord will give grace and glory: no good thing will he withhold from them that walk uprightly. O Lord of hosts, blessed is the man that trusteth in thee.

Whenever you reject your self-will, you will always desire the presence of God. You will be willing to hear from him in any decision before you conclude on anything and you will have time for God thereby allowing his Spirit to help you and your desire change will come.

Self-will is what will prevent you from spending time with the lord, it will always remind you that the service in the church is taking much time than suppose, it will not allow you to worship God because it will cause you doubt the promises of God in your life, by presenting a fake future or alternative way to you in order to trap and keep you bound forever.

Luke 4 v3-4: And the devil said unto him, If thou be the Son of God, command this stone that it be made bread.

And Jesus answered him, saying, It is written, That man shall not live by bread alone, but by every word of God.

Note'! Whatsoever the devil or the world has to offer you today is to take away your glorious desire change and Son ship from you

John 10v10: The thief cometh not, but for to steal, and to kill, and to destroy: I am come that they might have life, and that they might have it more abundantly.

Devil's offer will kill, steal and destroy you like in the case of Adam. God gave Adam the whole garden to take care of but the only gift that devil gave to him destroys him.

Devil always present his gift in your self-will to deny you the opportunity of listing to the voice of the

Holy Spirit, because he knows that your blessing or whatsoever you desire is in obeying the Holy Spirit.

Hannah could not please God until she listens to the voice of the Holy Spirit and change her prayer topic and ask in–line with the will of Holy Spirit whose interest is only to promote the Kingdom of God.

If Hannah had known all these years that her desire change will simply be given to her by only asking in-line with the will of the Holy Spirit or by accepting God's change first, she would not have waited for such a long time to receive Samuel.

Whenever you are willing to change your position and give up your self-will to do the will of the Holy Spirit by asking to promote the kingdom of God first, God will change your situation and give you a change that will cause you to rejoice and all those your neighbors that you wanted to revenge will be attracted to know your God. They will be won to back to God and that is the only reason, that God is giving you the change in any of your situation.

When your neighbors are won back to the kingdom of God where you belong, the room for revenge will no longer be there rather you will understand that all things work together for the glory of God in your life and you will show them mercy like in the case of Joseph and his brothers.

God does not want you to destroy your enemies when he gives you your desire change and that is why he cannot give it to you if you are asking in your self-will. "as it is written that recompense no man evil for evil"

So many Christians has stopped their desire change because they are having it in their mind, that as long as they live that any day God will do this or that for them, that they will use it to fight or boast against somebody that has belittle and offended them. They are saying this because of their unforgiving heart (self-will)

They have vowed not to let go no matter how long the incident has happened, they are still keeping it in their heart to revenge and pay back evil one day.

And that is why God has not given them their desire change because is not in-line with his plan. The word of God said that the blessing of the Lord makes rich and add no sorrow. All you need is to agree to change from your self-will to the will of God and your desire change will come.

When God see that sincerely you have change and your prayer topic has changed, then he will release your desire change to you.

Stop listing to the voice that will tell you that it is impossible to obey and do the will of God in every situation as a human being.

> *Matthew 26v39: And he went a little further, and fell on his face, and prayed, saying, O my Father, if it be possible, let this cup pass from me: nevertheless not as I will, but as thou wilt.*

Jesus set aside his fleshly desire to do the will of the father, Self-will will not allow you to see the glory ahead of you. Just sit down and consider the great glory that our Lord Jesus would have lost had it been that he agreed with devil and yield to his self-will.

For you to be able to overcome and receive your desire change you must be ready to say like our Lord Jesus! Oh Lord not my will but let your will be done and you will let your self-will to go away and the glory will appear.

> *Job 3 6v11: If they obey and serve him, they shall spend their days in prosperity, and their years in pleasures.*

God created everything for your good and He is not ready to take it away or withhold it from you but self-will takes them away from you. Refuse self-will for the glory (your desire change to appear) to appear.

Chapter Four

STOP EATING FROM THE ENEMIES TABLE

Many Christians today are under caves like the prophets in the time of Obadiah that was kept bound in a secret place so that they could no longer perform their assignments as prophets of God.

> *1Kings 18 v3-4: And Ahab called Obadiah, which was the governor of his house. (Now Obadiah feared the Lord greatly: For it was so, when Jezebel cut off the prophets of the Lord, that Obadiah took an hundred prophets, and hid them by fifty in a cave, and fed them with bread and water.)*

These prophets could not perform their duties, not because they are false prophets but because Obadiah was feeding them from the table of their enemy and for that reason they became silent, hiding in a cave without praying, making it impossible for the change their desire to come.

This is another method that devil and his agents are using to keep many children of God bound and stop them from receiving their desire change from God.

This method is also called Jezebel Spirit by the word of God. This spirit will not allow you to pray, it will keep you bound if you are eating from their table.

> *Revelation 2v19-26: I know thy works, and charity, and service, and faith, and thy patience, and thy works; and the last to be more than the first. Notwithstanding I have a few things against thee, because thou sufferest that woman Jezebel, which calleth herself a prophetess, to teach and to seduce my servants to commit fornication, and to eat things sacrificed unto idols. And I gave her space to repent of her fornication; and she repented not. Behold, I will cast her into a bed, and them that commit adultery with her into great tribulation, except they repent of their deeds. And I will kill her children with death; and all the churches shall know that I am he which searcheth the reins and hearts: and I will give unto every one of you according to your works. But unto you I say, and unto the rest in Thyatira, as many as have not this doctrine, and which have not known the depths of Satan, as they speak; I will put upon you*

> *none other burden. But that which ye have already hold fast till I come. And he that overcometh, and keepeth my works unto the end, to him will I give power over the nations:*

This spirit only allows evil works and stand against the will of God.

> *John 15v19: If ye were of the world, the world would love his own: but because ye are not of the world, but I have chosen you out of the world, therefore the world hateth you.*

Jesus made this statement as to wider your understanding to understand that you should not expect the world to love and encourage you for your good works instead bear in mind that the world will hate and try to discourage you the moment begin to speak up against evil, they will call you so many names just to discourage you, you might be treating with death when you refuse to bow to pressure and accept their corrupt way of doing things because the Jezebel spirit ruling the world will not be happy to see you as a child of God in right standing with God.

> *John 16v33: These things I have spoken unto you, that in me ye might have peace.*

> *In the world ye shall have tribulation: but be of good cheer; I have overcome the world.*

But Jesus said in the face of this calamity you should not be discouraged rather rejoice because he has already overcome the world and will give you the power to overcome them too if only you can make up your mind to stand firm in your faith in him.

> *Isaiah 60 v13: Arise, shine; for thy light is come, and the glory of the Lord is risen upon thee. For, behold, the darkness shall cover the earth, and gross darkness the people: but the Lord shall arise upon thee, and his glory shall be seen upon thee. And the Gentiles shall come to thy light, and kings to the brightness of thy rising.*

Meaning that God will give you a great victory whenever you refuse the food from enemy's table and choose to stand firm for God, he will give you victory that will cause you to be glorified above your enemies and problems.

> *Ephesians 4v17-19: This I say therefore, and testify in the Lord, that ye henceforth walk not as other Gentiles walk, in the vanity of their mind, Having the*

> *understanding darkened, being alienated from the life of God through the ignorance that is in them, because of the blindness of their heart: Who being past feeling have given themselves over unto lasciviousness, to work all uncleanness with greediness.*

Rejecting the food from your enemy's table and stay connected to the spirit of God will help you not to live in flesh, of which the work of the flesh is considered as a food from the enemy's table is which he served to keep you bound and make you not to receive your desire change.

> *Galatians 5v19-21: Now the works of the flesh are manifest, which are these; Adultery, fornication, uncleanness, lasciviousness, Idolatry, witchcraft, hatred, variance, emulations, wrath, strife, seditions, heresies, Envyings, murders, drunkenness, revellings, and such like: of they which I tell you before, as I have also told you in time past, that they which do such things shall not inherit the kingdom of God.*

All the works of the flesh as mentioned in the above scripture are the instruments or weapons that the devil and his agents use to feed you as child of God to keep you bound in a cave so that you will be silent and cannot fight the Jezebel spirit, thereby making it impossible for you to receive your desire change.

> *2 Corinthians 2v11: Lest Satan should get an advantage of us: for we are not ignorant of his devices.*

The word of God wants you to understand how the devil and his agents work by taking advantage of your ignorant using the works of flesh (enemy's food) to keep you silent and rob you of your desire change in life.

Note! Any sin or works of the flesh you are comfortable enjoying to the point where you cannot pray against it, is what the devil will use to destroy your spiritual life, hold you bound, disconnect you from God thereby making your desire change impossible whenever you are waiting upon God to bless you.

> *Galatians 5v16-17: This I say then, Walk in the Spirit, and ye shall not fulfil the lust of the flesh. For the flesh lusteth against the Spirit, and the Spirit against the flesh: and these are contrary the one*

> *to the other: so that ye cannot do the things that ye would.*

Any prayer topic (characters found in lust of flesh) that you cannot open your mouth wildly and pray against, means that the demons controlling such character is still living in you and their work is still killing you, stealing your blessing and destroying your spiritual life.

Whatsoever food that you are eating from the enemy's table that you cannot pray against is the best weapon that devil is using against your life and destiny.

Whatsoever thing that devil created is a weapon against the children of God to rob them their relationship with God and their desire change in life.

> *Revelation 2v19-20: I know thy works, and charity, and service, and faith, and thy patience, and thy works; and the last to be more than the first. Notwithstanding I have a few things against thee, because thou sufferest that woman Jezebel, which calleth herself a prophetess, to teach and to seduce my servants to commit fornication, and to eat things sacrificed unto idols.*

Understand also that Jezebel spirit is seduction spirit, very reproductive and it has many children, which the bible classified them as the works of flesh

> *Galatians 5v19-21: Now the works of the flesh are manifest, which are these; Adultery, fornication, uncleanness, lasciviousness, Idolatry, witchcraft, hatred, variance, emulations, wrath, strife, seditions, heresies, Envyings, murders, drunkenness, revellings, and such like: of the which I tell you before, as I have also told you in time past, that they which do such things shall not inherit the kingdom of God.*

> *1corinthians 6v9-10: Know ye not that the unrighteous shall not inherit the kingdom of God? Be not deceived: neither fornicators, nor idolaters, nor adulterers, nor effeminate, nor abusers of themselves with mankind, Nor thieves, nor covetous, nor drunkards, nor revilers, nor extortioners, shall inherit the kingdom of God.*

> *Ephesians 5v5-7: For this ye know, that no whoremonger, nor unclean person,*

nor covetous man, who is an idolater, hath any inheritance in the kingdom of Christ and of God. Let no man deceive you with vain words: for because of these things cometh the wrath of God upon the children of disobedience. Be not ye therefore partakers with them.

1Timothy 1v9-10: Knowing this, that the law is not made for a righteous man, but for the lawless and disobedient, for the ungodly and for sinners, for unholy and profane, for murderers of fathers and murderers of mothers, for manslayers, For whoremongers, for them that defile themselves with mankind, for men stealers, for liars, for perjured persons, and if there be any other thing that is contrary to sound doctrine;

As we have seen all the characters that the scripture classified as the works of the flesh, let's take them one after another, understand that any of these sins that you are still holding so dear to the point that you cannot let it go, is classified as food from enemy's table, prepare and serve by Jezebel spirit that is looking for a means to keep you bound and destroy you.

And is only when you reject this food of the enemy that you can be able to speak up against them in prayer as Elijah did during the time of Jezebel's wicked act, while other prophets were hiding comfortable and they are complaining because of Obadiah's food that always come from the enemy's table,

If you ask so many Christians they will tell you plainly that they are not happy the way our society, churches, organizations, associations, schools is been managed by our leaders but because of food from enemy's table they cannot speak up against the evil system.

> *Proverbs 15v17: He that is greedy of gain troubleth his own house; but he that hateth gifts shall live.*

Today so many Christians cannot tell their boss the gospel or ask them to repent from their sinful life because of enemy's food which makes them to be afraid of losing their job, even when they know that speaking up or preaching Christ at this point is the best thing to do as the bible said that he that win a soul is wise but they will choose to be foolish, eat from the enemy's table to avoid losing their position.

Most Christians are afraid to tell their friends, boss, and mates that smoking or fornication is sin because it destroys the temple of God which is their body.

Seeing government making laws and policies that are against the will of God, nature and you will keep silent because you are eating from such policy and at such you cannot speak up or preach against it even the church knowing that such law or policy is against the will of God.

> *Romans 8v19: For the earnest expectation of the creature waiteth for the manifestation of the sons of God.*

Whenever you reject the enemy's food you will speak up against the works of the flesh, your desire and change will come to you.

Chapter Five

REMEMBERING YOUR TESTIMONIES

Forgetting to remember their testimonies are another reason that keeps many Christians bound and stopped them from receiving their desire change.

Many Christians easily forget their testimonies of miracle which the Lord has done previously in their lives, thereby provoking the Lord to anger which takes away the face of God from them and their heaven will be closed.

Whenever you forget all your testimonies which the Lord has done in your life yesterday, your faith will be destroyed today and you will find it very difficult to receive another miracle which is your desire change from the Lord, because you will lack faith to keep believing God.

Hebrews 11v6: But without faith it is impossible to please him: for he that cometh to God must believe that he is, and that he is a rewarder of them that diligently seek him.

So if God is not pleased with you, how can you he bless you or grant your desire change to you?

"He that must come to God must believe that he is the rewarder of that seek for him; meaning you have to remember what he has done before and believe that he can do it again.

Without you remembering what the Lord has done before in your life, his goodness, loving kindness, total protection, provision, healing etc., it will be impossible for you to trust him with all your heart that he can do new thing.

> *Matthew 15 v 7-9: Ye hypocrites, well did Esaias prophesy of you, saying, This people draweth nigh unto me with their mouth, and honoureth me with their lips; but their heart is far from me. But in vain they do worship me, teaching for doctrines the commandments of men.*

You might be serving God but whenever you forget your testimonies, God will consider you unworthy to entrust with his new blessing. You will be considered as one of those people that honored him with their mouth while their heart is far from him.

Meaning that you may be crying unto God for a change with your mouth and your heart will be saying a different thing, because you fail to remember great things and victory that he has done in your life in the past.

Forgetting your testimonies are a very big mistake that devil will trick you to do as a child of God in order to hider you from receiving your desire change.

Devil knows that your new testimony (Blessing) is attached to your old testimonies, so he will try everything within his power to make you forget your old testimonies whenever you are looking unto God for another testimony.

He will make you start complaining about the ones you have not received from God. He will give you some many reasons why it will be impossible for God to do it now, making you to believe that is too late, legally impossible and scientifically impossible or not yet time.

Devil knows that the moment you starts remembering your testimonies of what the Lord has done before in your life, your heart will be glad and it will lift your faith, making God to be well pleased with you and you must see a good reason to believe on him and glorify him and he will give you your heart desire.

Psalms 77 V 1-20: I cried unto God with my voice, even unto God with my voice;

and he gave ear unto me. In the day of my trouble I sought the Lord: my sore ran in the night, and ceased not: my soul refused to be comforted. I remembered God, and was troubled: I complained, and my spirit was overwhelmed. Selah. Thou holdest mine eyes waking: I am so troubled that I cannot speak. I have considered the days of old, the years of ancient times. I call to remembrance my song in the night: I commune with mine own heart: and my spirit made diligent search. Will the Lord cast off for ever? and will he be favourable no more? Is his mercy clean gone for ever? doth his promise fail for evermore? Hath God forgotten to be gracious? hath he in anger shut up his tender mercies? Selah. And I said, This is my infirmity: but I will remember the years of the right hand of the most High. I will remember the works of the Lord: surely I will remember thy wonders of old. I will meditate also of all thy work, and talk of thy I will meditate also of all thy work, and talk of thy doings. Thy way, O God, is in the sanctuary: who is so great a God as our

God? Thou art the God that doest wonders: thou hast declared thy strength among the people. Thou hast with thine arm redeemed thy people, the sons of Jacob and Joseph. Selah. The waters saw thee, O God, the waters saw thee; they were afraid: the depths also were troubled. The clouds poured out water: the skies sent out a sound: thine arrows also went abroad. The voice of thy thunder was in the heaven: the lightnings lightened the world: the earth trembled and shook. Thy way is in the sea, and thy path in the great waters, and thy footsteps are not known. Thou leddest thy people like a flock by the hand of Moses and Aaron.

So many Christians has formed the habit of forgetting their testimonies whenever they found themselves facing any little challenges in their lives that they desire a change on and that will lead them to forget what the Lord has done before in their life.

From the above scripture David declared that he was mediating on the year of right hand of God, meaning he was always mediating on his great deliverance and mighty works which the Lord has done to his people in the past.

And this habit of mediation made David to always trust God at all-time even in hopeless situation, he will believe that God must do something and cause deliverance to his people and David his servant.

This habit made God to say that David is a man after my heart. Before any victory that God gave to David during his days, you will see that David will first of all start boasting in the name of God, telling the situation in face that God did this and he did that before and he is going to deliver me in your hand now.

Afterward, he will tell God in his testimony that you have done more than this before and I know that you can do it again. Instead of complaining he will praise God for the ones he has done before and that will cause God to do more.

We see this during his great challenge with Goliath. We see that no man was able to face Goliath in the camp of the Israelites; when Goliath's presence discouraged and makes the heart of the entire Lord's army to faint because all the people of God fail to remember the testimonies of what God has done in the past.

They all forgot the whole might works that God did in the history of his people, how he divide the red sea and how he gave his people victory through King Saul victory over the same Philistines a few years back . All these testimonies of what God has done in the past vanished from their minds, simply because they are facing a new challenge and their desires for change cause them to forget their old testimonies.

But thank God for a young David who did not forget his past testimonies and God gave him victory because he chooses to show class unlike King Saul and all his armies that quickly forget the great victory of the Lord in time past.

David's remembering of mighty works that the Lord has done in the time past and boasted with that in front of the whole people without shame caused the Lord to deliver Goliath into his hand.

> *Matthew 10 v 33: But whosoever shall deny me before men, him will I also deny before my Father which is in heaven.*

"Jesus said if you are ashamed of me in front of the people, I will be shame of you too in the presence of my father"

So many people that are looking unto God hoping to receive their desire change are ashamed to share their last testimony in the church or to tell people what the Lord has done in their life before.

David boasted with the name of God and God has to answer him without further delay, He remembered that God said I am the Lord and my glory I will not share with any man"

Do not allow your situation to share the glory of God in your life, never allows the Devil to blind your eyes, so that you begin to question the goodness and his existence in your life whenever you are faced with any challenge in life.

> *Psalm 78v10-20: They kept not the covenant of God, and refused to walk in his law; And forgat his works, and his wonders that he had shewed them. Marvellous things did he in the sight of their fathers, in the land of Egypt, in the field of Zoan. He divided the sea, and caused them to pass through; and he made the waters to stand as an heap. In the daytime also he led them with a cloud, and all the night with a light of fire. He clave the rocks in the wilderness, and gave them drink as out of the great depths. He brought streams also out of the rock, and caused waters to run down*

like rivers. And they sinned yet more against him by provoking the most High in the wilderness. And they tempted God in their heart by asking meat for their lust. And they tempted God in their heart by asking meat for their lust. Yea, they spake against God; they said, Can God furnish a table in the wilderness? Behold, he smote the rock, that the waters gushed out, and the streams overflowed; can he give bread also? can he provide flesh for his people? Therefore the Lord heard this, and was wroth: so a fire was kindled against Jacob, and anger also came up against Israel; Because they believed not in God, and trusted not in his salvation:

Imagine the great miracles of protection, provision, preservation that the children of Israel enjoyed from God, only to went ahead and limits his power because of a little challenge that came across their way and they asked can "God furnish a table in the wildness".

Anything that will make you to limit God's power in face of any problem you are facing in life, is capable of killing you. Whenever you are facing any challenges or bad situation of any sort and you begin to act as if the situation is beyond God's power, know that Devil is out to rob you of your desire change and will destroy you as well.

And this can only be possible when you forget your testimonies and all that the Lord has done for in the past. Forgetting your testimony will give room for the devil to introduce his sinful means of solving the problem to you which will destroy you in the long run.

Understand that is the original plan of the devil for you to take this sinful step, knowing very well that you will fail at long run because your strength will not be enough to fight him when you take this measure as the Bible said that by strength shall no man prevail.

Forgetting God's blessing will make you not to value God's blessings in your life. Many people that are crying for change in their marriages have not sat down once to thank God for making that marriage available for them in the first place, forgetting that lots of people out there are only looking for partner spend their life with.

Complaining about your marriage when others are only looking for whom to marry or who will marry them or agree to spend the rest their life with, is a means of provoking God to anger. A lots of people that are believing God in the area of promotion in work, have not sat down to thank God for providing the job for them in the first place, when millions of people are jobless, forgetting that their job is a miracle that only God can do thereby God desire to be praise first and thank before asking for another.

Some people that wants change in the lives of their children, complaining that they have stubborn children, have fail to sit down and thank God for providing such a wonderful gift, as the bible said that children are gift from the lord, knowing full well that a lots of people are childless, These kind of people knows very that children are inheritance from God and they are still complaining thereby provoking God to anger.

Many people that want material change such as cars, furniture, computer accessories etc., have not sat down and thank God for providing the current ones that they are using before asking for a change from God.

> *Isaiah 59 v1-3 Behold, the Lord's hand is not shortened, that it cannot save; neither his ear heavy, that it cannot hear: But your iniquities have separated between you and your God, and your sins have hid his face from you, that he will not*

hear. For your hands are defiled with blood, and your fingers with iniquity; your lips have spoken lies, your tongue hath muttered perverseness.

Understand that to receive your desire change from the Lord is simple. God cannot hide any good thing from his people but the mystery to receive it lays in your thanksgiving or remembering your testimonies.

Luke 17 v 11-19: And it came to pass, as he went to Jerusalem, that he passed through the midst of Samaria and Galilee. And as he entered into a certain village, there met him ten men that were lepers, which stood afar off: And they lifted up their voices, and said, Jesus, Master, have mercy on us. And when he saw them, he said unto them, Goshew yourselves unto the priests. And it came to pass, that, as they went, they were cleansed. And one of them, when he saw that he was healed, turned back, and with a loud voice glorified God, And fell down on his face at his feet, giving him thanks: and he was a Samaritan. And Jesus answering said, Were there not ten cleansed? but where are the nine? There are not found that returned to give glory to God, save this stranger. And he said unto him, Arise, go thy way: thy faith hath made thee whole.

Jesus healed ten lepers that have been expecting God for this desire change all the days of their lives.

All the days of their lives these men have been crying for God to change their condition. And by the grace of God they met Jesus who healed them and ask them to go and show themselves to the High priest. They went and were confirmed clean.

The news of their heal spread abroad but these people went and began to celebrate with families, friends and forget to come back and thank God that has healed them.

The Bible said that only one of them remember his testimony and came back to thank Jesus for healing him while the other nine were nowhere to be found they prefer to give the glory of God to their lustful desire.

So many Christians are like these nine lepers, they only want God to change their situation so that they will go back to their sinful way and manner of living.

In fact, the only reason they come to God is because they want to deceive God by receiving from him and go back to celebrate with the world.

> *Romans 12 v 2: And be not conformed to this world: but be ye transformed by the renewing of your mind, that ye may prove what is that good, and acceptable, and perfect, will of God.*

The bible warned us not to conform with activates of this world because the love of this world is enmity with God.

Whenever you remember your testimonies you see reason to value what God has done therefore appreciate his work in your life, like the case of the one of those 10 lepers that remembered his testimony and came back to thank Jesus, which prompt Jesus to bless him the more and restore whatsoever he has lost as result of his sickness.

God has many more blessing that he still want to give to you, if you can remember and value his past work in your life. In fact all the desire change you are looking for has been freely given to you in Christ

> *1 Corinthians 2v12: Now we have received, not the spirit of the world, but the spirit which is of God; that we might*

> *know the things that are freely given to us of God.*

All you need is just to sit down and remember your old testimonies appreciate his past works and thank him for the ones he has done to you in the past and the Holy Spirit will reveal your blessing to you and you will freely enjoy whatsoever change you desire in life.

Your desire change is possible, just search your mind to remember your past testimonies, take your time to consider all his good works in your life, then appreciate him as the miracle worker and he will do more.

Understand that you are where you are now by the grace of God and not by your power, where you are today, many people out there are praying to God so that they can be there but God chooses to place you there. Note! That whatsoever you have before looking for a change now, is someone's praying point.

God has made you a role model in that your situation to millions of people that wishes to be like you. So appreciate God first and he will cause your heaven to open and grant you your desire change.

> *Revelation 12 v11: And they overcame him by the blood of the Lamb, and by the*

> *word of their testimony; and they loved not their lives unto the death.*

Use your past testimonies to overcome every bad situation that you desire to receive change. Overcoming by the word of their testimony means applying the Word of God wisely to every situation you face.

Remember that Satan does not want you to understand or believing your position in Christ. Because he knows that your position in Christ grants you all authority over every demonic attack that Satan wants to launch against you. Your testimony grants your change to you without further delay.

Chapter Six

GIVING TO YOUR PROPHETS

Giving to your Prophet is another way to attract your desire change speedily. In fact, your desire change is tied to your Prophet.

> *2 Chronicles 20 v 20: And they rose early in the morning, and went forth into the wilderness of Tekoa: and as they went forth, Jehoshaphat stood and said, Hear me, O Judah, and ye inhabitants of Jerusalem; Believe in the Lord your God, so shall ye be established; believe his prophets, so shall ye prosper.*

Shows that your prosperity in any area begins the moment you believe your Prophet. Your desire change starts from obeying the word of God from the mouth of his Prophet.

Many people today are tied down by devil and his agents because they fail to receive and give to a Prophet. Receiving to a Prophets means given to a Prophets either to support his ministry or for his personal up keepings in the name of a Prophet

Jesus made this remark that whosoever gives to a Prophet a cup of water in the name of a prophet will receive a Prophetic reward, why because Prophets are God's agent or instruments of Change. The anointing of God upon the life God's Prophets turns impossibility to possibility, every situation are turnable to God's Prophets because they has the word of God on them.

> *John 10 v34-35: Jesus answered them, Is it not written in your law, I said, Ye are gods? If he called them gods, unto whom the word of God came, and the scripture cannot be broken;*

They always stand in a gap as a god to change a cause in any condition in your life and the way you treat them determines how your prosperity will treat you.

To be frank, you cannot be successful in life without a Prophet of God by your side; the truth is simple because there is no how that God can reach out to help you without a Prophet.

Meaning for you to receive your desire change from God, somebody must represent God as his agent (Prophet) at any moment to carry out God assignment that will cause that change to reach you. Take note of this, there must always be an agent to act for your fulfillment or the change at any point in time.

Your ability to reorganize your Prophet is your gateway to receive your desire change from God. Because whenever you obey him you can no longer fail because the Prophetic Spirit will not fail, it carries the divine presence of God for change.

God must send his Prophets to preserve your life in times of trouble. Understand that in times of troubles, sickness, poverties, and barrenness, sorrow and other challenges in life, God cannot come physically deliver you rather he will use somebody to work.

During the time of Israelite's suffering in Egypt God said I have come to deliver them because their crying has come unto me, meaning he has already answered their prayers but they were not liberated by that statement only, because God is a Spirit and he need's human agent to send because Spirits does not operate physically on earth without a physical vessels.

> *Psalm 115 v 16: The heaven, even the heavens, are the Lord's: but the earth hath he given to the children of men.*

God's search for human agent to send leads him to found Moses, who stood as a Prophet in the place of God to deliver his people.

Understand that God might have understood your problem or what you are passing through and might have answered your prayer and send his agents to meet your need but not until you discover and reorganized these agents, you might not be delivered or receive your desire change.

> *Hosea 4v6: My people are destroyed for lack of knowledge: because thou hast rejected knowledge, I will also reject thee, that thou shalt be no priest to me: seeing thou hast forgotten the law of thy God, I will also forget thy children.*

Many people have rejected the Prophets and agents that God send to deliver them out of Ignorance because of their lack of knowledge about the word of God and that has caused them to keep suffering in penury.

Seeking to discover you're Prophet, is very important whenever you are facing any difficulties of any sort in life that you desire change. So in times of trials all you need as a child of God is to ask him to reveal your Prophet or agent of change whom he as sends to deliver you at that moment to you.

> *Matthew 7v7-8: Ask, and it shall be given you; seek, and ye shall find; knock, and it shall be opened untoyou: For every one that asketh receiveth; and he that seekethfindeth; and to him that knocketh it shall be opened.*

Jesus gave this assurance because he knows that God can never abandon you when seek to know anything from him, including seeking to know your Prophet.

Mind you, Prophets are not people that will tell you about your past, your future and your problems without solution rather God's Prophets are those that understand your problems and have instant solution to it. That is God's standard of a Prophet.

> *Matthew 12 v 25-26: And Jesus knew their thoughts, and said unto them, Every kingdom divided against itself is brought to desolation; and every city or house divided against itself shall not stand: And if Satan cast out Satan, he is divided against himself; how shall then his kingdom stand?*

A lot of people today are claiming to be Prophets but they are false Prophets that are using diabolical means to operate, they may know your problem but they cannot solve it, rather they will compound the problems the more for you.

The bible called these types of people wolves in sheep cloth, they are working for the kingdom of darkness; they have demons in them and therefore cannot fight against their fellow demons.

John 10 v10: The thief cometh not, but for to steal, and to kill, and to destroy : I am come that they might have life, and that they might have it more abundantly.

So be warn and never to consider this type of people as Prophets else they will destroy you.

> *2 peter chapters 2 v 1-3 But there were false prophets also among the people, even as there shall be false teachers among you, who privily shall bring in damnable heresies, even denying the Lord that bought them, and bring upon themselves swift destruction. And many shall follow their pernicious ways; by reason of whom the way of truth shall be evil spoken of. And through covetousness shall they with feigned words make*

> *merchandise of you: whose judgment now of a long time lingereth not, and their damnation slumbereth not.*

Apostle Peter said they will make merchandise of you. To know real Prophets or God's agents, the bible said by their fruity you shall know them. God's Prophets has the mind of God in them. They have the Holy Spirit in them and the fruit of the Holy Spirit must be seen in their activities and character at all time. Galatians 5 v22-24: But the fruit of the Spirit is love, joy, peace, longsuffering, gentleness, goodness, faith, Meekness, temperance: against such there is no law. And they that are Christ's have crucified the flesh with the affections and lusts.

> *John 12 v49-50 : For I have not spoken of myself; but the Father which sent me, he gave me a commandment, what I should say, and what I should speak. And I know that his commandment is life everlasting: whatsoever I speak therefore, even as the Father said unto me, so I speak.*

Jesus was talking about the Holy Spirit upon his life, which is the Spirit of the father and Prophets has the same Spirit in them: when they speak they speak from the mind of God and God must perform it because it is his Spirit that speaks through his Prophet and he cannot deny his word.

So whosoever that tells you your whole problems without solution is not Prophesying to you in the name of God but whosoever that prophesy to you in the name of God and it comes to pass believe him because of that word of God and fruit of the Holy Spirit that is reflecting in his character.

And whenever you discover that somebody is a Prophet of God, understand that it is expected of you to give to him, so as to receive from him your desire change without delay. Whenever you are in a difficult situation or tight corner and God open your eye to discover a Prophet, know that he wants you to give to the Prophet in order to receive your desire change.

Many Christians will complain that I am poor or wise as such they don't want to hear the gospel of giving to your Prophet because the fail to understand that the gospel of giving to a Prophet is the perfect will of God.

Some may ask this questions; why must the poor that is looking for a means of survival or how to take care of his family give to a rich Prophets or a man of God that has enough already. These people are asking these questions because of their little knowledge about what the word of God said on this issue.

These are the people that God said they perished because of their lack of knowledge to understand that the foolishness of God is far wiser than man's wisdom.

The mystery there is that by so doing the poor will give himself out of poverty.

> *Luke 4 v 18-19 The Spirit of the Lord is upon me, because he hath anointed me to preach the gospel to the poor; he hath sent me to heal the brokenhearted, to preach deliverance to the captives, and recovering of sight to the blind, to set at liberty them that are bruised,To preach the acceptable year of the Lord.*

What the poor needs from the Prophet is the gospel and not money. The gospel there is that the poor or someone that needs change should take care of the Prophet first and by so doing he will receive his desire change.

And God knows that it will be difficult for the poor to give but whenever you give as a poor person or in your difficulties God will multiply whatsoever you give and give it back to you in more folds. The mystery is that by giving to a Prophet you receive it in more folds.

If you can understand the mysteries behind giving to your Prophets, you will develop the habit of giving to your Prophets.

> *Hebrews 7v8: And without all contradiction the less is blessed of the better. And here men that die receive tithes; but there he receiveth them, of whom it is witnessed that he liveth. And as I may so say, Levi also, who receiveth tithes, payed tithes in Abraham.*

Show that whatsoever you give to God's Prophets, you give to God. Whenever you see a Prophet, see him as a God that you are seeing at that moment. He represents God in your situation.

God said to the Moses to tell the children of Israel that I am has come when he sent him to deliver them thereby making him (Moses) God before them.

So whatsoever you want to give to God give it to them, giving to them attracts God's blessings in your life. You must see your Prophets as a God and whatsoever he said take it as what God said and whenever you see him, see him as someone that has something to offer.

Like the woman of Zarephath who was confused at the cross road of her life and God sent Elijah to sustained her. What Elijah did was to preach the gospel and the woman's change came forth. So if you think that you are poor means you need good news from a Prophet that will attract your desire change

You cannot say that you are too poor that you don't have something to give if you are sincere you will know that you have something to give to God and you have to give it to his agents (Prophets) to attract your desire change.

> Luke 21 v1-4: And he looked up, and saw the rich men casting their gifts into the treasury. And he saw also a certain poor widow casting in thither two mites. And he said, Of a truth I say unto you, that this poor widow hath cast in more than they all: For all these have of their abundance cast in unto the offerings of God: but she of her penury hath cast in all the living that she had.

Jesus made this remark that a poor widow that gave her last mint, gave out of her poverty. So don't allow the devil to tell you that you are too poor or that your condition is so bad that you cannot give.

It is when you are poor or in needy that you need to give out of your poverty for God to release his blessing to you.

Jesus was speaking he said that if you are faithful in little you will be trusted with much. The amount or what you give does not matter, what matters is how faithful you are. It is in your deepest poverty that you will receive blessing or desire change, if you give to a Prophet.

> *Philippians 4v10-12: But I rejoiced in the Lord greatly, that now at the last your care of me hath flourished again; wherein ye were also careful, but ye lacked opportunity. Not that I speak in respect of want: for I have learned, in whatsoever state I am, therewith to be content. I know both how to be abased, and I know how to abound: every where and in all things I am instructed both to be full and to be hungry, both to abound and to suffer need.*

Apostle Paul said that these people gave out of their poverty and they are willing to give more to his ministry and he prays for them in verse 19 of the same Chapter, asking God to supply them with both physical and spiritual change.

So for you to succeed and receive your desire change in your life, you have to discover and submit to your Prophet because your Prophet knows what you don't know and his information is spiritual and is based on what God is saying at that moment.

> *Hebrews 7 V7: And without all contradiction the less is blessed of the better.*

You might gather all your human information but understand that God cannot do anything without revealing it to his Prophets. So discovering instant or particular information or answer to a particular situation from God must be on your dependent to your Prophets, because he will tell you whatsoever thing he receives from God at any moment.

To receive your desire change faster, you need to discover your Prophet and believe him for your change to come.

Chapter Seven

YOU ARE QUALIFIED

Another way to receive your Desire Change from God is having the mindset or ability to discover and understand that you are qualified to receive such change from God.

Even when everybody seems not notice you or things are turning tougher in spite of all your efforts and nothing seems to change, don't be discouraged, and just have the mindset that you are qualified to receive your desire change, no matter how tough the challenges around you might seem.

Understanding that you are qualified or that you have meet the basic requirement needed to receive such change from God will motivate and position you in the right track to receive your desire change from God.

Coming to the knowledge to understand that God has placed a basic requirement on any change you desire here in life and that he is willing to give it to you whenever you meet that requirement.

> *Matthew 7 v7-11 Ask, and it shall be given you; seek, and ye shall find; knock, and it shall be opened unto you: For*

every one that asketh receiveth; and he that seeketh findeth; and to him that knocketh it shall be opened. Or what man is there of you, whom if his son ask bread, will he give him a stone? Or if he ask a fish, will he give him a serpent? If ye then, being evil, know how to give good gifts unto your children, how much more shall your Father which is in heaven give good things to them that ask him? God is a loving father and is willing to give you your desire change as soon as you discover that you are qualify to receive such change

1 Corinthians 2 v12: Now we have received, not the spirit of the world, but the spirit which is of God; that we might know the things that are freely given to us of God.

He has given you all things free in Christ Jesus, thereby making it your inheritance to have any change you desire but on condition of mirth only. Meaning that you can only receive any change you desire whenever you are qualified for such change.

Jesus said that only a sick person needs a doctor. Meaning as healthy person you might not urgently need a doctor. Because as a healthy person you do not need healing of any sort, thus a healthy person is not qualified for healing. If you desire's healing as the desire change that you want from God, you must first of all accept that you are sick before asking for healing.

So many Christians today has succeeded in keeping themselves in sick bed for long time out ignorance of this mystery. They know very well that they are sick but keep confessing that they are not sick; they called this kind of confession positive confession. Understand that such positive confession might keep you long time in your sick bed.

> *2 Corinthians 8 v 9: For ye know the grace of our Lord Jesus Christ, that, though he was rich, yet for your sakes he became poor, that ye through his poverty might be rich.*

The scripture above said that Christ was made poor, so that we might be rich through his poverty. Meaning Christ poverty is what qualifies you to be made rich in all things. Thus making his poverty a tool of your glory, Christ was made poor so that God through his poverty might change our poverty to his riches.

Stop allowing the devil to keep deceiving you in the name of positive confession

> *Colossians 1 v 26-29: Even the mystery which hath been hid from ages and from generations, but now is made manifest to his saints: To whom God would make known what is the riches of the glory of this mystery among the Gentiles; which is Christ in you, the hope of glory: Whom we preach, warning every man, and teaching every man in all wisdom; that we may present every man perfect in Christ Jesus: Whereunto I also labour, striving according to his working, which worketh in me mightily.*

Devil will always tell you to keep confessing that you are rich even when poverty is written all over your body. A lot of Christians has been taught to always confess positively even when the situation is against them in the name of positive confession and that is plan of the devil to keep you bound without allowing you receive your desire change.

Listen I am not against confession of faith as the scripture said that God will do whatsoever he hear you say as his servant, still you have to understand that not all closing doors are from devil.

> *Romans 8 v 28: And we know that all things work together for good to them that love God, to them who are the called according to his purpose.*

It takes the spirit of God as the above scripture said those who works not after flesh, when you are in Spirit as a child of God you will come to the rightful knowledge of God where you will understand that not all closing doors come from the devil and that they are not made to destroy you rather to qualifies you for the blessing of God.

> *Hosea 4 v 6: My people are destroyed for lack of knowledge: because thou hast rejected knowledge, I will also reject thee, that thou shalt be no priest to me seeing thou hast forgotten the law of thy God, I will also forget thy children.*

The bible also warned that you should not be ignorance of the divest of the devil because devil understood that the moment you discover and understand that your poverty is qualification to be rich in Christ that God will reveal to you how or what it takes for you to be rich, so he will not allow you to accept that you are poor rather he will deceive you into confessing that you are rich in name of positive confession and that is why things are not changing in your life. Devil know that without you accepting your poverty statue first you are not qualified to be made rich, without accepting that you are sick first, you are not qualified to receive healing.

A lot of people are facing tough times, struggling from one problem to another that needs God's deliverance but devil has blind their eyes, thereby denying them the understanding to know that they are qualified to receive deliverance from God by their sitution

> *Hebrews 11v35 Women received their dead raised to life again: and others were tortured, not accepting deliverance; that they might obtain a better resurrection:*

And these kinds of people are under demonic torment because they refuse deliverance by believing the teaching of Jesus that only the sick needs doctor. They know that something is wrong in their life but they refused to pass through deliverance. And in reality all is not well with them but they believe that when it comes to deliverance unbelievers are to be called.

Devil will not allow them to understand the mystery behind asking God for a change without receiving the change even after applying the whole bible principle as " ask you shall receive" is because they have come short of this knowledge and mystery of mirth or qualification.

They have come short of the knowledge that every blessing has qualified people to receive it. Example; for you to be healed you must be sick, for you to be set free from bondage you must be oppressed, making all things works for good for you because you are the called according to the purpose of God.

So understand that whatsoever situations you are passing through in life that is making you look unto God for a change is not made to destroy you rather to qualify you into receiving your desire change.

> *Joel 3 v 10: Beat your plowshares into swords, and your pruninghooks into spears: let the weak say, I am strong.*

The bible said let the weak said I am strong and not the strong say I am strong, meaning that you have to accept first that you are weak before been qualified to receive God's strength.

Devil has lied to many Christian that God can never answer their prayers because of their past sin and whenever they knee down to pray devil will bring the picture of such sin or their past to accuse them even after they might have asked God for forgiveness

> *Romans 8v 14-18 For as many as are led by the Spirit of God, they are the sons of God. For ye have not received the spirit of bondage again to fear; but ye have received the Spirit of adoption, whereby we cry, Abba, Father. The Spirit itself beareth witness with our spirit, that we are the children of God: And if children, then heirs; heirs of God, and joint-heirs with Christ; if so be that we suffer with him, that we may be also glorified together. For I reckon that the sufferings of this present time are not worthy to be compared with the glory which shall be revealed in us.*

Devil will not allow them to enjoy their salvation and liberty in Christ, even when God has forgiven them of their sins.

> *2 Corinthians 5 v21; For he hath made him to be sin for us, who knew no sin; that we might be made the righteousness of God in him.*

The bible said that Jesus was made sin for us, to qualify us to obtain the righteousness of God. Making you the express image of the God's righteousness which far better than justified by faith only. But because Devil as the accuser of the brethren will not allow you to come to this mystery to understand what your situations qualifies you to receive from God rather he will use it as an arrow of limitation to cage you down.

But God expect you to tell the devil in his face whenever he came with such arrow to accuse you or tell you that God cannot answer you because of your past sin, that it is what qualifies you to be forgiven; remind him that Jesus died for sinner like you and that if not because of that sin you would not be qualified to be saved and that because of that sin God has forgiven and accept you back as his son.

> *Romans 8 v 10-17: And if Christ be in you, the body is dead because of sin; but the Spirit is life because of righteousness. But if the Spirit of him that raised up Jesus from the dead dwell in you, he that raised up Christ from the dead shall also quicken your mortal bodies by his Spirit that dwelleth in you. Therefore, brethren, we are debtors, not to the flesh, to live*

> *after the flesh. For if ye live after the flesh, ye shall die: but if ye through the Spirit do mortify the deeds of the body, ye shall live. For as many as are led by the Spirit of God, they are the sons of God. For ye have not received the spirit of bondage again to fear; but ye have received the Spirit of adoption, whereby we cry, Abba, Father. The Spirit itself beareth witness with our spirit, that we are the children of God: And if children, then heirs; heirs of God, and joint-heirs with Christ; if so be that we suffer with him, that we may be also glorified together.*

Do not allow the devil to keep deceiving you from not applying the word of God. When God's word said "give and it shall be giving back to you" the devil will not want you to give, so he will tell you that if you give this money that the pastor will use it to enrich himself and that you will not receive anything because the pastor might not be speaking from the mind of God, because he knows that for you to come out of poverty that you need to give because your giving will qualify you to receive from God.

The reason for giving you all these excuses is to prevent you from giving because he knows that you will be qualified for open heaven. The bible said that sowing time and harvest time shall never cease but devil will try to mislead you into believing that to sow in the house of God is to waste your money just to stop your harvest.

> *John 8 v 44 : Ye are of your father the devil, and the lusts of your father ye will do. He was a murderer from the beginning, and abode not in the truth, because there is no truth in him. When he speaketh a lie, he speaketh of his own: for he is a liar, and the father of it.*

The word of God called the devil father of all liars, meaning that whatsoever the devil say to you as a child of God is to steal from you and to discourage you and makes you unqualified to receive your desire change.

Whenever he is speaking to you from this direction just look forward to the other direction you will understand what he wants to steal from you.

Jesus said to the devil get thee behind me when he understood that the devil wants to steal his son -ship,

Christ discovered that devilish offer to him is not based on love but to steal greater glory from him.

So for devil telling you not to pay your tithe is not because he wants to help you grow financially but because he knows that the moment you are faithful in paying your tithe you will be qualified for total open heaven and that is why he can never allow you to pay your tithe, to make sure that you will not be qualified to receive your desire change.

In whatsoever problem you are passing through as a child of God, do not complain, just look at the problem from the angle of God's own point of view and you will understand that it is made to qualifies you and not to destroy you and without it God can never intervene.

Whenever you discover that your problems or what you are struggling in life is for your glory you will see more reason why you should thank God each new day and your complains will cease because you will understand that your condition is positioning you to receive your desire change.

> *Hebrews 12 v 2: Looking unto Jesus the author and finisher of our faith; who for the joy that was set before him endured the cross, despising the shame, and is set*

down at the right hand of the throne of God.

With the mentality that my condition is what qualifies me to receive my desire change, you will accept your condition first and understand that your sickness is what qualifies for healing; your broken heart is what qualifies for healing; your poverty is what qualifies you for riches; your jobless situation is what qualifies a call up; your disappointment is what qualifies you for an appointment; your sorrow is what qualifies to be console; your sin is what qualifies to be forgiving, your barrenness is what qualifies to convince.

So no matter what you are passing through today, thank God that you are passing through that situation and it's what qualifies to receive your desire change.

Romans 8 v 28: And we know that all things work together for good to them that love God, to them who are the called according to his purpose.

Chapter Eight
GROWING FROM A CHILD TO A SON OF GOD

To grow from a child of God to a son of God is another way to receive your desire change speedily.

> Romans 8 v 16-17 :The Spirit itself beareth witness with our spirit, that we are the children of God: And if children, then heirs; heirs of God, and joint-heirs with Christ; if so be that we suffer with him, that we may be also glorified together.

The above scripture made it open that as long as a heir reminds a child that there is no difference between him and a servant. Meaning the secret of the kingdom can never be given to him at that point because he is considered to be unfit to receive his inheritance.

No loving father will allow his three years old son to lay hand on any of his private or important documents such as check book, international passport etc. even when any of these documents rightfully belong to the child. The father can never allow the child to have access to it or use any of them on his own at this point because the father understands that the child can never handle them well as child because he does not know the value of such property.

Base on this reason the father will make it point of duty to keep those documents away from the child for so many years till when the child will grow to a maturity to understand the important and value of such documents before the father will comfortable release the documents or information pertaining to his business knowing full well now that child has grows be called a son and can now take good care of whatsoever the father commits into his hand.

And the father can now look boldly into his face and called him my son. Because he knows that his son has gone through many tough times and trials and proof himself worthy before growing into full man thereby will understand what the father requires from him. He will now see himself with the same eyes that the father sees him and will never disappoint the father, because he has allowed the will and technique of the father to transform him.

> *2 Corinthians 3 v18. But we all, with open face beholding as in a glass the glory of the Lord, are changed into the same image from glory to glory, even as by the Spirit of the Lord.*

That is why the bible said that we should train up a child in a way he should go, which he will not depart when his old. That is how our relationship with our heavenly father is. The bible declares that everything you need has been given to you in Christ Jesus, meaning that whatsoever you need is yours in Christ Jesus already and God has made them available for you to enjoy.

But the truth is that you cannot access those blessing out of ignorance as a child, so God has to keep them back till you grow from a child to a son where God your heavenly father will have confidence that you are capable of handling whatsoever that you want him to committee into your hand.

The bible also considered a child a servant who though might have served his master faithfully for so many years but cannot be considered worthy to receive or inherit the master's property by right and he cannot be called a son no matter how faithful he served the master.

> *Genesis 15 v 2-3: And Abram said, Lord God, what wilt thou give me, seeing I go childless, and the steward of my house is this Eliezer of Damascus? And Abram said, Behold, to me thou hast given no*

> *seed: and, lo, one born in my house is mine heir.*

Meaning only sons are qualified to receive the inheritance without struggling.

> *Romans 8v16-17: The Spirit itself beareth witness with our spirit, that we are the children of God: And if children, then heirs; heirs of God, and joint-heirs with Christ; if so be that we suffer with him, that we may be also glorified together.*

> *John 1v 12: 2 But as many as received him, to them gave he power to become the sons of God, even to them that believe on his name:*

The moment you accept Christ as you Lord and personal savior, God has adopted into the family of his dear son and has made provisions for you as his child to have every good thing as pertaining to this life as his child.

And it is his perfect will for you have all your desire change before ever asking for them. Before you knee down to pray God your heavenly father knows your heart desire. " As the spirit makes intercession for us" *1 Corinthians 3 v 2 1 Therefore let no man glory in men. For all things are yours;*

This universe and everything on it, is part of God's kingdom. "Heaven, even Heavens belong to God, the earth has he given to the sons of men"

You have to understand that heaven is the spiritual part or portion of God's kingdom. God's purpose is to create a spiritual family for his only begotten son Jesus Christ that will uphold and established righteousness and justice forever on earth.

> *Ephesians 1 v 5: Having predestinated us unto the adoption of children by Jesus Christ to himself, according to the good pleasure of his will,*
>
> *Romans 8v 14: For as many as are led by the Spirit of God, they are the sons of God. For ye have not received the spirit of bondage again to fear; but ye have received the Spirit of adoption, whereby we cry, Abba, Father. The Spirit itself beareth witness with our spirit, that we are the children of God: And if children, then heirs; heirs of God, and joint-heirs with Christ; if so be that we suffer with*

him, that we may be also glorified together.

Romans 8v23: And not only they, but ourselves also, which have the firstfruits of the Spirit, even we ourselves groan within ourselves, waiting for the adoption, to wit, the redemption of our body.

Romans 9v24-26: Even us, whom he hath called, not of the Jews only, but also of the Gentiles? As he saith also in Osee, I will call them my people, which were not my people; and her beloved, which was not beloved. And it shall come to pass, that in the place where it was said unto them, Ye are not my people; there shall they be called the children of the living God.

Galatians 4v4-7: But when the fullness of the time was come, God sent forth his Son, made of a woman, made under the law, To redeem them that were under the law, that we might receive the adoption of sons. And because ye are sons, God hath sent forth the Spirit of his Son into your hearts, crying, Abba, Father. Wherefore thou art no more a servant, but a son; and if a son, then an heir of God through Christ.

And to be part of this family start from believing in the name of Jesus Christ thereby making yourself available for God to adopt you into his spiritual family from the earth by the grace of whom he had made all provision where the desire change of this his spiritual family will be given freely.

The Psalmist said that he gave the earth to his sons of which you are part of them to inherit soon as you grow to become a son in the family. Understand that your heavenly father wants you to have all your desire change without problem or struggling. He confirms this when the scripture declare *"that whatsoever you ask the father in the name of the son, you shall receive them"*

It is very important to know that Jesus is talking to every son of the father on earth who is his co-heir on earth and this assurance is not to children in the family or babies.

Because as a baby you do not know your right, therefore it will be impossible for a baby to receive what he asks for. As a child can wake up from sleep and say to the father "daddy buy a lorry for me, if you are going back from work today" He asked this without considering that before driving this lorry that he needs a driving licenses, parking space etc. Though the father might answer yes but that does not mean that the father will buy the lorry why coming back from work rather the father might choose to buy him some toys or ice-cream in place of his demand.

That is the same way between baby Christians and God. Baby Christian will always ask foolishly and God will answer the pray because of his son. "Who sit at the right hand of the father" God will answer the pray but will give you what he knows that is fits for the child at the moment and not what child ask for.

James said that you cannot receive exactly what you asked for because you ask amiss.

Your problem as a baby Christian that refused to grow is not about asking or answering of the prayer but the problem is receiving exactly what you asked for:

And the ability to receive exactly what you ask for, lays only when you ask rightly and must have grown from a child to a son to know the right thing to ask and what the father has for you and ready to obey the father at all time, thereby making him happy at all time.

Now the question is "how can one grow from a child of God to a son of God" I assumed many people might have asked this question over and over in life.

The word of God said that as many that believe in his name, he gave them the power to become the children of God, first is to believe totally in Christ Jesus which is the word of God made flesh. When you believe you will be adopted into the family of God and growth start the moment you start eating the word of God, by studying and making it standard for your life, you will start growing from strength to strength physically, spiritually, financially etc.

"Jesus said that you cannot add cubic to your height by thinking alone, meaning no idea from any source can increase you physically, spiritually, financially etc., making every human idea both the one you learn from school to be in vain without the word of God. So understand that whatsoever increase you want or anything that it takes for you have increase in any area of your life can only found in Christ which is the word of God.

> *Psalm 119 v 130 The entrance of thy words giveth light; it giveth understanding unto the simple.*

The word mingled with your spirit, is what it take to make you grow into what God wants you to be before you will receive your desire change. The word is the light of men, when it multiplies in you, it will bring you light. Any man without the word of God in him, do not have direction of the future and as a result is working darkness, he cannot see what the future holds for him. But with the word of God in your heart you are sure to make progress in life and grow in spirit.

> *2 Corinthians 3v18: But we all, with open face beholding as in a glass the glory of the Lord, are changed into the same image from glory to glory, even as by the Spirit of the Lord.*

Whenever you are studying the word of God, you are looking at yourself, your future, your health, your marriage, your generation, your business in God's mirror.

The power of God in his word will give you the ability live according to what it says concerning your situation and help to grow in spirit, that is what the word of God does, when it multiplies in your heart.

> *"Apostle Paul said be filled with the word of God. Romans 12v2 ;And be not*

> *conformed to this world: but be ye transformed by the renewing of your mind, that ye may prove what is that good, and acceptable, and perfect, will of God.*

By constant studying of the word of God, will cause you to grow to a level where you will get to understand that God wants you to keep making amendment and change each new day, that he wants you to be better today than yesterday, it means growing every day from one level to another level till you become full grown up man where he can be pleased with you and call you son. And say "this is my beloved son" and this can only happen by renewal of your mind through the word of God.

Romans12 v2: Don't copy the behavior and customs of this world, but let God transform you into a new person by changing the way you think. Then you will learn to know God's will for you, which is good and pleasing and perfect.

Whenever you renew your mind with the word of God each new day, you will grow to a level where you will always make rightful decision and good choices at all point in life. And your prayer will always be answered, because you will grow to a level where you will understand the mind of God at every point in time, knowing full well that you are not alone as a result of the good fellowship that you are enjoying with him as you work in union with him.

> *1 Corinthians 6 v17: But he that is joined unto the Lord is one spirit.and knowing that you come to him by new birth and so you are in him now.*
>
> *John 14 v 10-12: Believest thou not that I am in the Father, and the Father in me? the words that I speak unto you I speak not of myself: but the Father that dwelleth in me, he doeth the works. Believe me that I am in the Father, and the Father in me: or else believe me for the very works' sake. Verily, verily, I say unto you, He that believeth on me, the works that I do shall he do also; and greater works than these shall he do; because I go unto my Father.*

Jesus enjoyed the same fellowship with the father and that is how he wants you to grow into a level where you will be conscious of whom you are, knowing that you a son of God and that you are not alone because the father dwells in you through his Holy Spirit.

> *Ephesians 5 v18-20: And be not drunk with wine, wherein is excess; but be filled with the Spirit; Speaking to yourselves in psalms and hymns and spiritual songs, singing and making melody in your heart to the Lord; Giving thanks always for all things unto God and the Father in the name of our Lord Jesus Christ;*

As many that are leads by the spirit of God are the sons of God. Whenever you are filled with the Holy Spirit means no more fear, no more worries of any kind, no more darkness, no more lack of direction in life, no more heart failure, no more lack, no more marriage crises etc. because you are the in Christ the express image of God.

> *Colossians 1 v 10-20 :That ye might walk worthy of the Lord unto all pleasing, being fruitful in every good work, and increasing in the knowledge of God; Strengthened with all might, according to his glorious power, unto all patience and longsuffering with joyfulness; Giving thanks unto the Father, which hath made us meet to be partakers of the inheritance of the saints*

in light: Who hath delivered us from the power of darkness, and hath translated us into the kingdom of his dear Son: In whom we have redemption through his blood, even the forgiveness of sins: Who is the image of the invisible God, the firstborn of every creature: For by him were all things created, that are in heaven, and that are in earth, visible and invisible, whether they be thrones, or dominions, or principalities, or powers: all things were created by him, and for him: And he is before all things, and by him all things consist. And he is the head of the body, the church: who is the beginning, the firstborn from the dead; that in all things he might have the preeminence. For it pleased the Father that in him should all fullness dwell; And, having made peace through the blood of his cross, by him to reconcile all things unto himself; by him, I say, whether they be things in earth, or things in heaven.

And whatsoever that is your heart desire will come because you are a son of God and all your steps will be directed by him and his Holy Spirit will review whatsoever mystery behind any problem to you as a son and you will have solution to your issues. "Because at the presence of God every issues of life are settled, you will have solution to all your problems "because as he is in heaven if so you are on earth.

You are his Ambassador, you rightful represent him on earth. So make up your mind today and grow from a child a son and you will see your desire change following you about.

> *Mark 16v17-18 And these signs shall follow them that believe; In my name shall they cast out devils; they shall speak with new tongues; They shall take up serpents; and if they drink any deadly thing, it shall not hurt them; they shall lay hands on the sick, and they shall recover.*

Chapter Nine

FIGHT A GOOD FIGHT OF FAITH

Another way to receive your desire change is by fighting a good fight of faith. Hebrews 11v1

Example; when God said in his word that you are blessed, faith there is that word of God that said it, that same word of God is the substance and evidence that you are holding in your hand as a proof that you are blessed, even when it has not come to pass. It's like when you go to super market and shop for some television sets, they give you receipt and promise to deliver the item to you later in the week. The receipt is the evidence that you have bought a television set from the super market and you can boldly tell your friends that I just bought a new television set even when the television set is yet to be delivered to you. That is what the word means when the word said you are blessed beyond curse; the word of God that said it is your proof that you are blessed beyond curse by anyone and you can boldly repeat it to anybody when people ask how do you know, you simply said I have a proof and my proof is the word of God that cannot lie.

Your faith is your convention about the word of God and it takes your deeper knowledge and revelation of the word of God for you have faith "to be convinced" or for your faith to grow.

This deeper revelation and convention is what is called THE GRACE OF GOD and it is differs depending on how convince you are in any area. This deeper revelation and knowledge about God is the grace of God upon your life that will convince you to believe and be convinced in the word of God.

It is this convention that made Abraham, when he received the word of God to believe God against nature.

> *Galatians 3 v6: Even as Abraham believed God, and it was accounted to him for righteousness.*
>
> *Romans 4v16-23 :Therefore it is of faith, that it might be by grace; to the end the promise might be sure to all the seed; not to that only which is of the law, but to that also which is of the faith of Abraham; who is the father of us all, (As it is written, I have made thee a father of many nations,) before him whom he believed, even God, who quickeneth the*

dead, and calleth those things which be not as though they were. Who against hope believed in hope, that he might become the father of many nations; according to that which was spoken, So shall thy seed be. And being not weak in faith, he considered not his own body now dead, when he was about an hundred years old, neither yet the deadness of Sara's womb: He staggered not at the promise of God through unbelief; but was strong in faith, giving glory to God; And being fully persuaded that, what he had promised, he was able also to perform. And therefore it was imputed to him for righteousness. Now it was not written for his sake alone, that it was imputed to him;

The same convention made Apostle Paul when he received the full revelation of the word of God to declare "that I can do all things through Christ which is the word made flesh.

Philippians 4v13: I can do all things through Christ which strengtheneth me.

For your faith to stand and grow strong in God, you must have this deeper knowledge of the word of

God in you that is why the bible said that faith cometh by hearing and hearing the word of God. When you understand that the word of God is the proof or evidence that you have at hand, whenever you hear the word of God you will be convinced that is true and what God is saying about me and whatsoever thing he said is final, you will be convince and believe him, thus your faith will grow because you know that as he has said it, he will do it and you will be willing to hear what he will tell you because you will be ready to believe whatsoever he said without doubt.

With a heart a man believes and mouth confession is made. The faith there is the convention that causes him to believe on Jesus that he never see in the first place, accepting that he died for him and confessing that he died for him with convention.

In the same manner if you have this kind of faith" convention" on anything you will receive it from God that is what faith is all about.

> *Romans 10 v10-13: For with the heart man believeth unto righteousness; and with the mouth confession is made unto salvation. For the scripture saith, Whosoever believeth on him shall not be ashamed. For there is no difference*

> between the Jew and the Greek: for the same Lord over all is rich unto all that call upon him. For whosoever shall call upon the name of the Lord shall be saved.

Jesus said that if you believe that you can say to this mountain be removed and the mountain will be removed and you cannot believe anything without been convince. For you to believe, you must be convinced that God is able to do that and that nothing is impossible for him to do and without this convention you can never attract God into action.

> *Hebrews 11 v 6: But without faith it is impossible to please him: for he that cometh to God must believe that he is, and that he is a rewarder of them that diligently seek him.*

Faith is your convention about God, the response of your human spirit to the word of God.

> *Matthew 12 v18-20: Behold my servant, whom I have chosen; my beloved, in whom my soul is well pleased: I will put my spirit upon him, and he shall shew judgment to the Gentiles. He shall not strive, nor cry; neither shall any man hear his voice in the streets. A bruised*

> *reed shall he not break, and smoking flax shall he not quench, till he send forth judgment unto victory. And in his name shall the Gentiles trust.*
>
> *Matthew 21 v21-22: Jesus answered and said unto them, Verily I say unto you, If ye have faith, and doubt not, ye shall not only do this which is done to the fig tree, but also if ye shall say unto this mountain, Be thou removed, and be thou cast into the sea; it shall be done. And all things, whatsoever ye shall ask in prayer, believing, ye shall receive.*

Without having this convention that nothing is impossible before Christ and believing that he was from the beginning and knows everything till the last

> *John 1 v 1-3 : In the beginning was the Word, and the Word was with God, and the Word was God. The same was in the beginning with God. All things were made by him; and without him was not anything made that was made.*

You cannot please God and attract him in your desire change, "because whosoever will come to him must believe that he is the rewarder of them the seek for him"

This deeper revelation and convention about him must come whenever Christ that is the word of God is living in you

> *2 Peter 1 v 19-21: We have also a more sure word of prophecy; whereunto ye do well that ye take heed, as unto a light that shineth in a dark place, until the day dawn, and the day star arise in your hearts: Knowing this first, that no prophecy of the scripture is of any private interpretation. For the prophecy came not in old time by the will of man: but holy men of God spake as they were moved by the Holy Ghost.*

Meaning that all you need to receive your desire change in life is your deeper revelation and knowledge of the word of God and be convince on it, accepting the word the way it says it then you will work in your high places and receive whatsoever desire you want from God.

Moreover devil will always want you to believe the negative side of your convention, he will keep bring negative side to you. Example when God said he has open a door that no man can close in your life through his word, then devil will remind you of your step mother, who is diabolic and has vowed that you can never succeed in life.

The reason for presenting this negative thinking is to divert your attention from the word of God that says he opened a door for you to your evil step mother or uncle. Devil wants you focus your attention on the thought that this person said that you will not succeed instead of holding unto the word of God that opens the door for you and enjoy your liberty rather devil wants you to start praying against your step mother, uncle etc. waiting to see them die before you can accept the open door. At this point, his trap and homework from the pit of hell is to distract you from focusing on what the word of God said about you.

The problem is not the devil or his agents, the problem are how to fight to be focus and convince towards the word of God. Devil wants you to use your precious time that you suppose to use for studying of the word of God and be convinced so that you can build your life from the word to be wasted in fighting him (devil) and his agents whom Christ has defeated over 2000 years ago.

Colossians 2 v14-15 Blotting out the handwriting of ordinances that was

> *against us, which was contrary to us, and took it out of the way, nailing it to his cross;And having spoiled principalities and powers, he made a shew of them openly, triumphing over them in it.*

Devil is not the problem his power has been destroyed and collected by Christ Jesus and given to you but devil only try to trick you into believing that you have problem and believe the devil has power.

> *Matthew 28 v 18: And Jesus came and spake unto them, saying, All power is given unto me in heaven and in earth.*

> *Mark 16 v 17-18: And these signs shall follow them that believe; In my name shall they cast out devils; they shall speak with new tongues; They shall take up serpents; and if they drink any deadly thing, it shall not hurt them; they shall lay hands on the sick, and they shall recover. So by believing in name of Christ with convention you can cast out devils.*

> *2 Corinthians 2 v11 Lest Satan should get an advantage of us: for we are not ignorant of his devices.*

Apostle understood the tricks of the devil and he warned you that you should not be ignorance of it rather he advises that you should fight a good fight of faith and not fight of devils and demon because they are not important any more, fighting the devils makes them unnecessary important.

He understood that the moments you got the real revelation of the word of God in any area and become convince, that such convention which is your faith will destroy, expose the work of devils and make him useless as Christ made open show of the devil and his agents

> *1 Timothy 6v12; Fight the good fight of faith, lay hold on eternal life, whereunto thou art also called, and hast professed a good profession before many witnesses*

Fighting a fight of faith is fighting to keep your mind focused and fame on God's word at all time, believing with convention every word you receive from God with your whole heart without complaining, is the greatest weapon against the kingdom of darkness.

And devil knows about this and that is why the devil is fighting to make you not to believe the word of God with convention because he wants to keep you in bondage forever. He wants you to believe that you have problem while the word of God will make you understand that you don't any problem or cause for alarm because God has made everything you desire available in Christ, which the word made flesh.

> *2 Corinthians 2 v11 Lest Satan should get an advantage of us: for we are not ignorant of his devices.*

Also you have understood that the devil will use mixed multitude in your members to fight your believe or convention, whenever you are fighting to keep your faith strong in the word of God.

> *Exodus 12 v 37-38: And the children of Israel journeyed from Rameses to Succoth, about six hundred thousand on foot that were men, beside children. And a mixed multitude went up also with them; and flocks, and herds, even very much cattle.*

> *Numbers 11 v 4-5: And the mixt multitude that was among them fell a lusting: and the children of Israel also wept again, and said, Who shall give us flesh to eat? We remember the fish, which we did eat in Egypt freely; the*

> *cucumbers, and the melons, and the leeks,*
> *and the onions, and the garlick.*

We understood that the children of God allowed mixed multitude to follow them out of the land of Egypt and the members of the mixed multitude made them to sin against God by murmuring against God, they gave the mixed multitude among them chance to speak to them thereby making their faith in God to wax coal.

The mixed multitude made them to lost faith in God and his Servant Moses by remembering them that they do eat flesh freely in Egypt and the mixed multitude fail to remind the people that they do eat the flesh in punishment and in bondage. This is the same weapon that devil is using today against the children of God and to destroy their faith.

Understand that the mixed multitude was not the children of God (Israel) but the seed of enemy among them which the children of Israel refused to deal with.

Whenever you choose to listen to the voice of your flesh which devil is using to speak in your heart your faith will be destroy, the voice of your flesh will always suggest evil to you and if you fail to deal with it at that any moment, the voice will grow and become strong imagination that will be against the will of God.

> 2 Corinthians 10 v 5: Casting down imaginations, and every high thing that exalteth itself against the knowledge of God, and bringing into captivity every thought to the obedience of Christ;

Devil knows that the only you can receive your desire change and come out of darkness is by convention about what the word of God said.

> Galatians 5v 19-21: Now the works of the flesh are manifest, which are these; Adultery, fornication, uncleanness, lasciviousness, Idolatry, witchcraft, hatred, variance, emulations, wrath, strife, seditions, heresies, Envyings, murders, drunkenness, revellings, and such like: of the which I tell you before, as I have also told you in time past, that they which do such things shall not inherit the kingdom of God.

> 2 Corinthians 10 v3-6: For though we walk in the flesh, we do not war after the flesh: (For the weapons of our warfare are not carnal, but mighty through God to the pulling down of strong holds;) Casting down imaginations, and every high thing that exalteth itself against the

> *knowledge of God, and bringing into captivity every thought to the obedience of Christ; And having in a readiness to revenge all disobedience, when your obedience is fulfilled.*

And for this reason, he sows the mixed multitude in your body the bible called it the lust of flesh, which war against your members to destroy your faith. Complaining is always in your members to bring your faith down. Devil know that whenever you allow any work of the devil to speak in your flesh your faith will go down and you will sin against God.

So the devil will always present them to you knowing very well that the moment you start listening to them, that your faith will be destroyed and you will start complaining and murmuring against God. His primary aim is to take your mind away from the word of God which is the only tools that has exposed the kingdom of darkness and the greatest weapon against devils.

God's word makes you what God said that he will make you, what it talks about you and change your life whenever you have the word inside your heart.

> *Romans 12 v2: And be not conformed to this world: but be ye transformed by the*

renewing of your mind, that ye may prove what is that good, and acceptable, and perfect, will of God.

God wants you to transform through his word, the word of God "Christ" has made open show of the devil and triumph over them,

Colossians 2v 14-17: Blotting out the handwriting of ordinances that was against us, which was contrary to us, and took it out of the way, nailing it to his cross; And having spoiled principalities and powers, he made a shew of them openly, triumphing over them in it. Let no man therefore judge you in meat, or in drink, or in respect of an holyday, or of the new moon, or of the sabbath days: Which are a shadow of things to come; but the body is of Christ.

Meaning the only material that can destroy the power of darkness and capable of setting you free, from demonic influence and grant you the deeper knowledge on how to overcome the devil and all his work is the word of God.

Mark 11 v 23 : For verily I say unto you, That whosoever shall say unto this

> mountain, Be thou removed, and be thou cast into the sea; and shall not doubt in his heart, but shall believe that those things which he saith shall come to pass; he shall have whatsoever he saith.

Jesus said that you can say to this mountain be thou remove if you believe. The golden rule there is believed but you cannot believe if you are not deeply convinced. Whatsoever you believe you must achieve.

> Matthew 28 v20: Teaching them to observe all things whatsoever I have commanded you: and, lo, I am with you alway, even unto the end of the world. Amen.

When Jesus made this statement, he was talking about the Holy Spirit which is the indwelling presence of the father been with you.

> John14 v16: And I will pray the Father, and he shall give you another Comforter, that he may abide with you forever;

The comforter which is also referred as the Spirit of truth will abide with you to teach you all things including how to be convinced and receive your desire change in marriage, business etc.

The sole reason why the father is sending his Holy Spirit is for you not to work in flesh but to be filled with the Holy Spirit in fight for your faith. So pray for the Holy Spirit that will help you win your fight of faith and to come into your heart.

Holy Spirit already loves you and wants to live in you, just to help you overcome every weakness in your faith don't forget that.

> *2 Peter 1 v12-13 Wherefore I will not be negligent to put you always in remembrance of these things, though ye know them, and be established in the present truth. Yea, I think it meet, as long as I am in this tabernacle, to stir you up by putting you in remembrance;*

Other Books By Evangelist Harrison Johnson Uche

www.ingramcontent.com/pod-product-compliance
Lightning Source LLC
Chambersburg PA
CBHW070112080526
44586CB00013B/1274